Symbols, Landmarks, and Monuments

The
Golden Gate
Bridge

Tamara L. Britton
ABDO Publishing Company

visit us at
www.abdopub.com

Published by ABDO Publishing Company, 4940 Viking Drive, Edina, Minnesota 55435.
Copyright © 2005 by Abdo Consulting Group, Inc. International copyrights reserved in
all countries. No part of this book may be reproduced in any form without written
permission from the publisher. The Checkerboard Library™ is a trademark and logo of
ABDO Publishing Company.

Printed in the United States.

Cover Photo: Digital Vision
Interior Photos: Corbis pp. 1, 5, 6-7, 9, 10, 11, 13, 15, 16, 17, 18, 22, 23, 24, 25, 27,
    28, 29; Getty Images pp. 8, 19, 26

Series Coordinator: Heidi M. Dahmes
Editors: Heidi M. Dahmes, Megan M. Gunderson, Stephanie Hedlund
Art Direction & Maps: Neil Klinepier

Library of Congress Cataloging-in-Publication Data

Britton, Tamara L., 1963-
    The Golden Gate Bridge / Tamara L. Britton.
       p. cm. -- (Symbols, landmarks, and monuments)
    ISBN 1-59197-835-1
    1. Golden Gate Bridge (San Francisco, Calif.)--Juvenile literature. I. Title.

 TG25.S225B68 2005
 624.2'3'0979461--dc22
                                                        2004054872

Contents

Golden Gate Bridge

The Golden Gate Bridge is the seventh-longest suspension bridge in the world. It stretches across a strait called the Golden Gate in California. The bridge links the city of San Francisco with Marin County.

The Golden Gate Bridge was built during the **Great Depression**. Officials encountered difficulties raising money for the project. Workers struggled against rough conditions, including strong winds and turbulent waters. Some lost their lives while building the bridge.

But, the workers pressed on and completed the bridge in 1937. Today, thousands of people use the Golden Gate Bridge to move freely across the strait. It is a landmark to those who sail under it in San Francisco Bay. And, it is a symbol of the determination and spirit of those who created it.

Fog often covers the San Francisco Bay area.

Fast Facts

√ Joshua Norton was an unsuccessful businessman in San Francisco during the gold rush. Later, he declared himself emperor of the United States and began printing his own money. In 1869, Norton became the first person to officially proclaim the need for a bridge across the Golden Gate strait.

√ Joseph B. Strauss was awarded $1 million and a lifetime pass across the Golden Gate Bridge for his successful completion of the project. He died less than a year after the bridge opened.

√ Riveters working on the Golden Gate Bridge's hollow towers sometimes became lost inside them for several hours.

√ In 1994, the American Society of Civil Engineers named the Golden Gate Bridge one of the Seven Wonders of the Modern World.

√ Today, the longest suspension bridge is the Akashi Kaikyo Bridge in Japan. It has a main span of 6,532 feet (1,991 m).

√ Every day, 118,000 cars cross the Golden Gate Bridge. That adds up to more than 40 million cars a year!

√ Eleven men were killed while removing wooden supports from beneath the paved roadway in 1937. The safety net collapsed, and they fell 220 feet (67 m) into the icy waters below.

Timeline

1846	√	John C. Frémont named the Golden Gate strait.
1847	√	The town of Yerba Buena changed its name to San Francisco.
1848	√	Gold was discovered at Sutter's Mill.
1872–1919	√	Several people submitted plans for a bridge across the Golden Gate strait.
1921	√	Michael O'Shaughnessy introduced a plan by Joseph B. Strauss.
1930	√	The U.S. War Department approved the plans for the Golden Gate Bridge.
1933	√	In January, construction on the Golden Gate Bridge began.
1936	√	On November 18, workers laid the last piece of roadway.
1937	√	On May 27, 18,000 people crossed the bridge on Pedestrian Day to celebrate the opening of the bridge.
1951	√	Officials scheduled the bridge's first repairs.
1972	√	The Golden Gate Bridge National Recreation Area was created.

The Golden Gate

Storms create rough seas near the Golden Gate Bridge.

California is the third-largest state in the United States. Shipping is an important part of California's **economy**. Ships enter and leave the San Francisco Bay area through the state's only major inlet.

This inlet is a deep channel that connects San Francisco Bay to the Pacific Ocean. In 1846, explorer John C. Frémont named this three-mile- (5-km) long strait. He called it the Golden Gate.

Water from two sources meets at the Golden Gate. The Sacramento and San Joaquin rivers empty into San Francisco

Bay. At the strait, fresh waters from the rivers mix with salt water from the Pacific Ocean. This creates strong, perilous currents in the strait.

In addition to rough waters, the Golden Gate strait has **unpredictable** weather. Strong, gusty winds and heavy fog often fill the air. Traveling through the Golden Gate can be difficult and unsafe.

Some people opposed the construction of the Golden Gate Bridge. They thought it would be unsafe, expensive, ugly, and most of all, harmful to the natural landscape.

A Growing City

Carpenter James W. Marshall discovered gold at Sutter's Mill in 1848.

To the south of the Golden Gate strait lies the San Francisco **peninsula**. There, settlers built the town of Yerba Buena in the early 1800s. In 1847, the town's name changed to San Francisco.

In 1848, about 800 people lived in San Francisco. That same year, John Sutter had a sawmill built east of the city along the American River. Soon, gold was discovered at Sutter's Mill. When word spread of the find, thousands of people rushed to the area.

San Francisco's population increased as **prospectors** arrived. Many prospectors bought the supplies they needed in the city. More merchants arrived to supply them. And, **stevedores** came to the port to unload the incoming goods. By 1850, nearly 35,000 people called San Francisco home.

In 1942, the California Park Service created the Marshall Gold Discovery State Historic Park. Today, visitors can pan for gold at a reconstruction of Sutter's Mill.

Many people who went to California did not find gold or become wealthy. However, **prospectors** often stayed in the San Francisco area to look for other jobs. Merchants remained successful because the population continued to grow.

In 1906, more than 300,000 people lived in the city. At the time, only eight American cities were larger. San Francisco's population grew to fill the **peninsula**. There was little space available to build more businesses and housing.

For this reason, people began to commute and take weekend trips across the Golden Gate strait. They made the trip on **ferries**. By the 1920s, 50,000 people used the ferries each week. The population continued to increase, so city planners worked to find a better way to cross the strait.

Opposite page: *Today, more than 776,000 people live in San Francisco. The San Francisco skyline is visible from the Golden Gate Bridge.*

Bridge Designs

Californians wanted to connect San Francisco to Marin County with a bridge. Most citizens knew that building a bridge would create jobs and improve the **economy**. It would also allow San Francisco's growing population to spread out. A bridge would benefit people on both sides of the strait.

In 1872, Charles Crocker gave city officials a bridge plan. In 1916, newspaper editor James H. Wilkins did the same. City planners agreed that a bridge across the strait was a good idea. However, there was no money for the project at that time.

Then in 1919, officials asked city engineer Michael O'Shaughnessy to develop a plan for a bridge. He asked several engineers to create plans. Joseph B. Strauss's plan cost less than those proposed by the other engineers. So in 1921, O'Shaughnessy introduced Strauss's plan to city officials.

Golden Gate Bridge Statistics

Total length of bridge: 8,981 feet (2,737 m)

Length of suspension span between towers: 4,200 feet (1,280 m)

Width of bridge: 90 feet (27 m)

Width of six-lane roadway between curbs: 62 feet (19 m)

Width of each of the two sidewalks: 10 feet (3 m)

Weight of each anchorage: 60,000 tons (54,431 t)

Weight of each tower: 44,000 tons (39,916 t)

Clearance above water: 220 feet (67 m)

Height of each tower above roadway: 500 feet (152 m)

Rivets in each tower: Approximately 600,000

Length of each main cable: 7,650 feet (2,332 m)

Cost to build the bridge today: $1.2 billion

Bridge toll 1937: 50¢

Bridge toll 2004: $5

Busiest day: October 27, 1989. After an earthquake closed the Bay Bridge, 162,414 vehicles crossed the Golden Gate Bridge.

Foghorns help ships navigate safely near the Golden Gate Bridge.

In 1923, the state legislature passed the Golden Gate Bridge and Highway District Act. This act created an association to raise money, get land, and build a bridge. In 1928, the association created the Golden Gate Bridge and Highway District to finance, design, and construct the bridge.

The U.S. War Department owned the land that engineers wanted to build the bridge on. War Department officials wanted to make sure the bridge would not get in the way of shipping through the strait. After much study, the department approved construction in 1930.

Strauss became the chief engineer. He hired Professor Charles Ellis as an engineering expert. Ellis and Leon Moisseiff created the bridge's design. And, Irving Morrow was hired as the **architect**.

Then, voters from the Highway District approved a plan to finance the bridge. They would allow the sale of **bonds**. But during the **Great Depression**, most people did not have extra money.

The bonds did not sell. So, Strauss asked banker Amadeo Giannini for a loan. Instead, the banker bought $6 million worth of bonds to finance the project.

Amadeo Giannini founded the Bank of America and the Transamerica Corporation.

Construction Begins

In 1931, Strauss fired Ellis. He thought Ellis was working too slowly and spending too much money. Strauss hired managing engineer Clifford Paine to replace him. In January 1933, construction on the Golden Gate Bridge began.

Strauss wanted the bridge workers to be safe. So, he hired Russell Cone as resident engineer. Cone **supervised** daily work and helped maintain safety for all workers.

Strauss and Cone required all workers to wear safety helmets.

Strauss also had a safety net put in place below the bridge during roadway construction. The net extended ten feet (3 m) on

Paine (left) *and Strauss* (right) *survey construction of the Golden Gate Bridge.*

Workers used special concrete to construct the anchorages. The concrete was made partly from crushed oyster shells from the floor of San Francisco Bay.

either side of the new bridge. This helped the builders work more quickly because they felt safe. The net would catch anyone who might fall into the raging waters below.

Support System

The first construction task was to build the bridge's 12-story **anchorages**. Workers dug huge pits and filled them with more than 1 million tons (900,000 t) of concrete. These concrete boxes held the bridge's main cables to the ground. So, the anchorages had to be strong.

For their second task, the workers built the bridge's piers. These are the concrete foundations that the towers stand on. The north pier was built next to the shore in only 20 feet (6 m) of water. It was finished quickly.

Common Elements of a Suspension Bridge

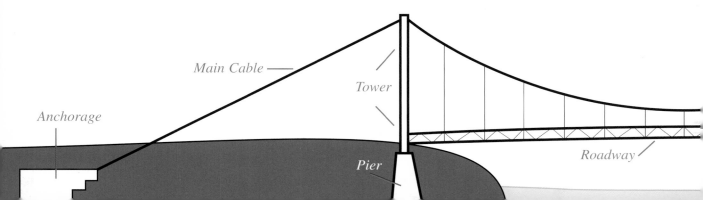

The south pier had to be built more than 1,000 feet (300 m) into the bay. First, divers worked on the seafloor. They dug holes, filled them with explosives, and blew them up. Next, they removed the debris.

Then, workers built a fender around the area where the pier would sit. It helped the workers build the pier. And, it kept the south tower safe from ships when the bridge opened.

Originally, Strauss planned to use a **caisson** inside the fender. But, the water was too rough. So, workers pumped the water directly out of the fender. This gave the men less protection. But, the workers safely poured the concrete foundations for the piers and let the water back in.

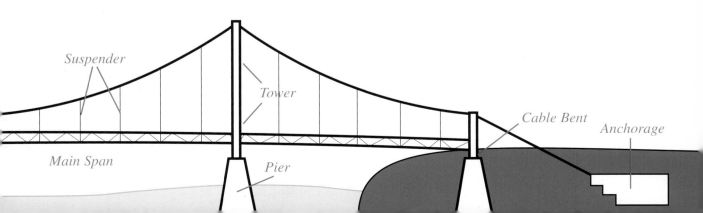

Suspender

Tower

Cable Bent

Anchorage

Main Span

Pier

The Towers Rise

When the piers were finished, workers could begin building the towers. The towers were designed in the sleek **art deco** style that was popular at the time. The steel for the towers was from Bethlehem Steel in Pennsylvania.

No one knows exactly how many people helped build the bridge.

The towers were designed to be hollow. Workers **riveted** together each piece of steel from the inside. This made the towers strong but light. The towers were 746 feet (227 m) high. By 1935, both towers were finished.

Next, workers needed to paint the steel towers to protect them from the harsh weather in the strait. People argued about which color to use. Some thought the bridge should be painted gray. The navy thought it should be black and yellow striped so that ships could see it more easily.

Architect Irving Morrow suggested International Orange. This color would contrast with the sky and blend in with the hills of Marin County. Eventually, everyone agreed with his suggestion. International Orange gave the Golden Gate Bridge the distinctive look it maintains today.

Workers completed the north tower first. The south tower was finished more than a year later.

Cable Network

The piers and towers were complete. Now, the bridge needed the cables that would attach a roadway to the towers. The John Roebling and Sons company was hired to construct the cables. Its experts had built the Brooklyn Bridge.

To do the cable work, the men built footbridges from one end of the bridge to the other. A complex system of weights, **pulleys**, and spinning wheels was also created. This system allowed cable to be run back and forth between the **anchorages**.

The cables of a suspension bridge transfer all the weight to the towers and anchorages.

The cables were spun from steel wire. The two main cables are about three feet (1 m) wide. Each one is

made up of 25,572 pencil-thin parallel wires. In all, 80,000 miles (128,748 km) of wire were used for the bridge's main cables.

These cables were wrapped with steel wire to protect them from the weather. So, each cable looks like one solid piece of steel. By working on the Golden Gate Bridge, John Roebling and Sons perfected their system. The bridge's cables were completed in only six months.

A Roadway at Last

Roadway construction was the last step. The roadway steel was also provided by Bethlehem Steel. The road is suspended from the two main cables by 254 sets of **vertical** cables.

On the afternoon of November 18, 1936, the last piece of roadway was laid. The final piece of steel was designed to fit only after it had warmed and expanded in the sun. The bridge finished $1.3 million under budget and only five months late.

San Franciscans held a weeklong celebration when the bridge was finished. On May 27, 1937, 18,000 people crossed the newly paved bridge. This was declared Pedestrian Day. Some

The roadway had to be built outward in equal distances. This kept the bridge in balance during construction.

By the end of 1985, 1 billion cars had crossed the bridge.

people competed to be the first person to walk across the bridge forward, backward, on **stilts**, or on roller skates.

The next day, President Franklin D. Roosevelt announced to the world that the bridge was open. By midnight, more than 30,000 cars had crossed from San Francisco to Marin County on the Golden Gate Bridge.

27

Suspension Success

The Golden Gate Bridge National Recreation Area is one of the most popular national parks in the country.

The Golden Gate Bridge has stood strong for more than 60 years. It has required few repairs. After a windy storm in 1951, workers strengthened the roadway with steel **girders**. In the 1970s, the **vertical** cables were replaced. And in 1985, the original road was replaced with asphalt and new steel.

Citizens appreciated the bridge as a transportation option. But, they also knew it was a thing of beauty. So in 1972, the Golden Gate Bridge National Recreation Area was created.

The recreation area has 75,398 acres (30,513 ha) of land and water. It has 59 miles (95 km) of bay and ocean coastline. Each year, almost 16 million people visit the area. Many enjoy bird-watching, boating, surfing, biking, camping, and hiking. All visitors delight in the breathtaking view of the bridge.

A painter attending to bridge maintenance

The Golden Gate Bridge was built during trying times, under harsh conditions, and in a challenging location. It has become more than a landmark. It is a symbol of the imagination, commitment, and determination needed to reach a difficult goal.

Glossary

anchorage - an object to which something may be fastened and held securely.

architect - a person who plans and designs buildings. His or her work is called architecture.

art deco - a style from the 1920s and 1930s that uses bold shapes and designs.

bond - a certificate sold by a government. The certificate promises to pay its purchase price plus interest on or after a given future date.

caisson - a large, waterproof structure used for underwater construction.

economy - the way a nation uses its money, goods, and natural resources.

ferry - a boat used to carry people, goods, and vehicles across a body of water.

girder - a level structural unit that supports an upright load, typically used in the construction of a building or bridge.

Great Depression - a period (from 1929 to 1942) of worldwide economic trouble when there was little buying or selling, and many people could not find work.

peninsula - land that sticks out into water and is connected to a larger landmass.

prospector - a person who searches for minerals, especially gold.

pulley - a wheel over which a rope or cable may be pulled to help heavy loads move or change direction.

rivet - to fasten with a bolt of metal, typically used to secure two beams into place.

stevedore - a person who loads and unloads cargo from ships.

stilt - a pole that has a footrest attached partway up from the bottom of the pole. Used in pairs, they allow a person to appear taller by walking with their feet above ground.

supervise - to watch over and take care of something.

unpredictable - something that cannot be guessed ahead of time.

vertical - in the up-and-down position.

Web Sites

To learn more about the Golden Gate Bridge, visit ABDO Publishing Company on the World Wide Web at **www.abdopub.com**. Web sites about the Golden Gate Bridge are featured on our Book Links page. These links are routinely monitored and updated to provide the most current information available.

Index